Our Lives, Our World

Spain

Chrysalis Children's Books

First published in the UK in 2004 by
Chrysalis Children's Books
An imprint of Chrysalis Books Group Plc
The Chrysalis Building, Bramley Road
London W10 6SP

Copyright © Chrysalis Books Group Plc 2004
Photography © Francisco Rodriguez, Marta Bustos
Cabeza, Encarni Vega Gallego and Desiree Barrios
Gil 2004

Compiled and edited by Susie Brooks
Editorial manager: Joyce Bentley
Designed by: Tall Tree Books Ltd
Photographic consultant: Jenny Matthews
Picture researcher: Jamie Dikomite
Translator: Anthony Leaker

ISBN 1 84458 090 3

Printed in China

10 9 8 7 6 5 4 3 2 1

British Library Cataloguing in Publication Data for
this book is available from the British Library.

The Publishers would like to thank the
photographers, Francisco Rodriguez, Marta Bustos
Cabeza, Encarni Vega Gallego and Desiree Barrios
Gil, for capturing these wonderful children on film.
Corbis: Pete Saloutos FCBL, 1, 29CR, 30B; Jon
Hicks 4BR; Hubert Stadler 5T; Patrick Ward 5BL;
Tony Arruza 9C; Charles & Josette Lenars 10TR;
Corbis Sygma 11BR.

Holt Studios: FC CL, 5TR.

Contents

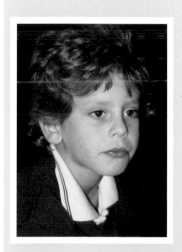

¡Hola! – Hello!

We are the children of Spain and we can't
wait to share our lives with you in this book!

Welcome to Spain!

We've got so much to show you. Let's start by telling you a bit about our country. We hope you'll come and see Spain for yourself some time soon!

Land and sea

Spain is in Western Europe. It is the second largest country there – only France, to the north, is bigger. Most of Spain is surrounded by sea. The Canary Islands and the Balearic Islands also belong to our country.

Holiday spot

Many people travel to the coasts of Spain to enjoy the sunny beaches.

Rocky border

There are mountains in the north and south of Spain. The highest are the Pyrenees, which run along the border with France.

Warm weather

Spain has a varied climate, cooler in the north than in the south. Central and southern Spain can get very hot in the summer. People living in Madrid, our capital city, often move out to cooler areas during the summer months.

National symbols

These are the yellow and red stripes of our country's flag.

Out and about

The Retiro Park in Madrid is popular at weekends. Families go there to relax in the open air and enjoy the attractive scenery.

Speak Spanish!

hola – hello

adios – goodbye

por favor – please

gracias – thank you

5

Francisco

Hi! I'm Francisco Bravo Vega and I'm 6 years old. I live with my mum and dad in the city of Málaga. Our house doesn't have a garden but it is close to some fields. I have one sister, Claudia – she's 22 and has left home to go to university.

'I am very cheeky and energetic. I like to run and jump about, and I also fall over a lot!'

Mum and dad look after me really well. They invent lots of games to entertain me and they make me laugh. I sometimes help mum with the housework, but that's not so much fun!

My sister and I are the best of friends. I really look forward to her visits in the holidays.

This is my pet dog Alba – he's a great playmate! I also have a cat called Lucky. You can see her in the picture at the top – she loves sitting on my lap!

I walk to school every morning – it's just down the road. I like learning, but my favourite time is 2.00 pm when we can go home!

Going to school

Until the age of 6, many children in Spain go to school only in the mornings. They arrive at 8.00 am or 9.00 am and finish at around 2.00 pm. Sometimes they have extra classes in the afternoons, such as dancing or sports. Older children finish at 5.00 pm but they often go home for a few hours at lunchtime.

Finishing school doesn't mean the day is over – we get homework to do in the afternoon!

After school I have lunch with my family. When the weather's good, we sit out on the terrace on the roof of our house.

For a treat, we go to a café like this one in the square.

My favourite dish is paella. It is made of rice cooked with seafood, meat and vegetables.

Eat and sleep

Lunch in Spain is often eaten late, at around 2.00 pm or 3.00 pm. Many people then have a rest, called a 'siesta'. Dinner is another late meal, which some families don't eat until 10.00 pm or 11.00 pm. Around the clock, many cafés serve snacks, called 'tapas'. These are small portions of different foods, including bread, olives, seafood, cooked meats and potatoes in delicious sauces.

After lunch I sometimes have a sleep. In the evenings I go to bed at 9.00 pm or 10.00 pm.

There is lots to see in Málaga. This is a view of the bullring where we sometimes go during festivals.

Bullfighting

Many towns and cities in Spain have a bullring, where fights are held between men and bulls. Bullfighting has been a traditional sport in Spain for hundreds of years. It is still popular today, though some people think it is cruel to the animals.

This is the theatre where my dad works. He belongs to the Málaga Municipal Band. When I'm older I would like to be a musician. I want to learn to play the violin.

The shops here stay open till late. I like wandering round the tourist stalls. In the photo below, I'm looking at prints of paintings by the famous Spanish artist Pablo Picasso.

Spending money

The money we use in Spain is called the euro. One euro is divided into 100 cents. We can use the euro in lots of different countries around Europe. Before the year 2002 we spent 'pesetas', which could only be used in Spain.

Maria

Hi! My name is Maria Olalla Ruiz and I am 7 years old. I live in Málaga with my mum, dad and brother Juan Luis who's 12. My family is the best thing in my life. Dad is always kidding around and telling jokes – he makes me laugh a lot!

'I don't have a pet – just my brother!'

I live in a lovely house with a big garden. We have our own swimming pool and a basketball court. Sometimes my neighbour Marta comes round to play.

There's a terrace on the roof of our house. We sometimes go up there to eat or relax. This is the view we see!

13

I love sports. At school I take karate classes - I'm the one in the red boots! The navy blue clothes are part of our school uniform. I'm also learning to rollerblade, but I still wobble a bit!

Sports

Sports are an important part of life in Spain. Schoolchildren take part in all sorts of activities, from basketball to karate and gymnastics. Football is one of the most popular games and lots of people support their local team.

I was given this toy electric guitar as a present. It's quite hard to play. I would like to be good enough to play in a band one day. Dance music is my favourite. I spend my pocket money on CDs, as well as toys...and sweets!

I love this sweet shop – it's opposite my house. I wish I could eat sweets instead of school lunches! Today we had rice soup and chicken nuggets.

My best friend Ana and I are doing a play at the local church (below left). We're learning about our religion, Catholicism. We go to classes every week and say prayers daily at school.

Religion

Although various religions exist in Spain, most Spaniards are Catholics. Many Catholic children are given lessons in the church to teach them about their faith. Their families may also take them to church every week to pray and receive a blessing.

After the play I join my family. You can see me with my parents and brother on the left of the picture and my aunt, uncle and cousins on the right. They live in Málaga, too.

16

One of my favourite times of year is the festival of Epiphany, when the Three Wise Men Parade comes to town. There are floats with clowns and children in costumes. They throw sweets and give us presents!

Fiestas

Spain is famous for its colourful festivals, called 'fiestas', that happen throughout the year. Many are based on the Catholic religion and celebrate holy days or the lives of different saints. Every part of Spain has its own typical fiesta. Most involve fancy dress parades, fireworks and feasts of traditional foods.

Ricardo

Hi there, I'm Ricardo Fernandez Vazquez! I'm 6 years old and I live in Benadalid, a village in the hills in the south of Spain. I have a sister, Salome, who's 8.

'When I grow up I'd like to be a vet because I want to look after animals.'

I love animals. We own a farm with dogs, cats, rabbits, sheep, chickens, goats, pigs and donkeys! It's in the countryside, about 15 minutes from our house.

This is my family. My dad runs a building company and my mum works with him.

I like pulling faces when Salome gives me a hug!

Our village is in a river valley. It is very small and quiet – only 300 people live here and there are hardly any cars. All the houses are white. Many have decorative plants hanging on the walls.

White villages

There are many mountain villages in this part of Spain. The sun can be very hot here. Houses are painted white to reflect the heat, keeping them cooler inside. Outside, people often hang up washing to dry in the heat. Desert plants like cacti grow well in this climate.

I go to school in the village. There are only 10 children in my class and 16 pupils in total. We do some of our lessons, such as this messy painting activity, outside in the playground.

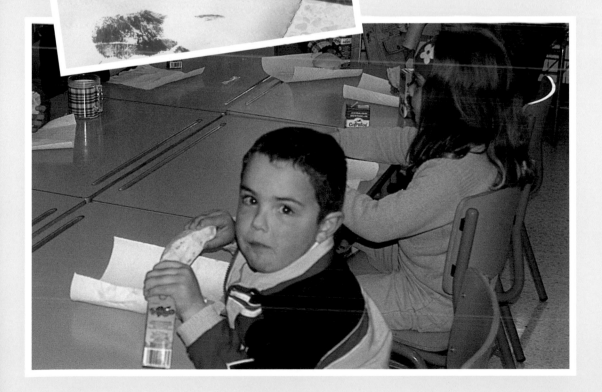

At 11.00 am we stop for our 'Andalucian breakfast'. We eat oven-baked bread with olive oil and salt. I really like it!

At school we are taught to plant trees. I like learning about nature and exploring the farms and countryside around our village.

These are the flowers of an almond tree.

And this is a grove of cork trees. The cork comes from the bark.

Farming

Spain's sunny climate is ideal for growing fruits, nuts and vegetables. Olives, almonds, chestnuts, figs and lemons are just some of the crops found here. Many village people own some land where they grow fruits and vegetables and raise animals such as sheep and chickens.

This is the branch of an olive tree.

Lemons and chestnuts are also grown around here.

Salome and I help out on the farm by feeding the chickens. They're eating leftovers from our lunch! A lot of our food comes fresh from the farm, including the chickens' eggs.

Li Da

Hello! My name is Li Da Zheng Chen. I am 6 years old and I live with my adopted family in Málaga. Our home is on the first floor of a block of flats and it looks out onto the sea. I really love living in Spain!

'I would like to get to know the whole of Spain. Most of all I'd like a house on the beach!'

This is the Spanish family that I live with. Paco, Juana and their two sons Jesus and Juan have looked after me ever since I was 2 months old.

My natural parents are from China but they live in Málaga. They gave me to Paco and Juana because they were not able to look after me themselves. I still see them for a short time every day. My brother Chen Xiu is 16 and goes to high school.

I'm very happy with my Spanish family. We have fun at mealtimes when we all sit together. Sometimes I invite my friends round, too.

Aunt Rosario is a great cook. She's teaching me how to make her special sauce – it's my favourite!

In the morning I like eating a traditional Spanish breakfast of bread with ham and olive oil.

Some other things I love about living here are...

going to the beach...   playing in the countryside...

...and shopping at the flower stalls around town!

My school is just 100 metres from my house. There are 500 pupils there, of 19 nationalities! This is the playground where we go at break time and for sports.

For today's homework I'm practising writing – it's my favourite subject! I read, write and speak Spanish at home and at school, and when I see my brother he teaches me Chinese.

Some afternoons I go to dance classes. I'm learning to dance flamenco and also to play the castanets. I wear a long, frilly skirt and special heeled shoes.

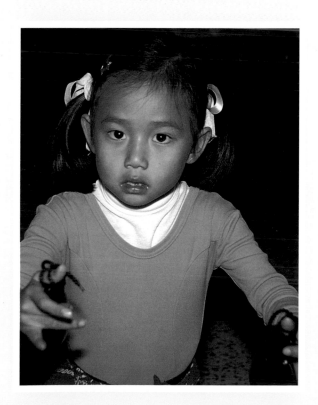

Flamenco

Flamenco is a type of music and dancing that is very famous in Spain. It was invented by gypsies in Andalucia hundreds of years ago. The dancers tap their feet and make graceful movements with their arms. They wear beautiful costumes and often hold an instrument called the 'castanets' which they click between their fingers.

Our Year

JANUARY

Epiphany In Málaga we watch the Three Wise Men Parade and receive presents and sweets.

Ricardo's birthday: 14 January

FEBRUARY

Carnival festivals All over Spain there are fancy dress parades, comedy shows and parties on the streets.

MARCH/APRIL

Easter school holiday: late March – mid April

Fire festivals In Valencia, huge handmade statues are paraded around and then burned.

Holy week A week of religious celebrations leading up to Easter.

April fair Flamenco parties, bullfights and horse shows take place in Seville.

MAY

Holy Cross In parts of Spain, people set up crosses and cones of fruit and flowers and sing, pray and dance around them.

Francisco's birthday: 20 May

JUNE

Li da's birthday: 17 June
Maria's birthday: 25 June

Corpus Christi Colourful processions and mystery plays take place around the country.

Summer school holiday: late June – end of August

JULY

San Fermin In Pamplona, men run through the streets in front of a herd of bulls, towards the bullring where a bullfight then takes place.

AUGUST

Tomatina In Buñol, Valencia, crowds throw squashed tomatoes at each other in a giant yearly food fight!

SEPTEMBER/OCTOBER

La Merce Barcelona comes alive with fireworks, parades, street theatre, human towers and dancing, in celebration of the city's patron saint.

NOVEMBER

All Saints Day Families remember the dead and eat traditional foods including biscuits, sweets and chestnuts.

DECEMBER

Christmas On Christmas Eve we go to church for midnight mass. We decorate our homes and exchange presents.

Christmas school holiday: late December – early January

¡Adios! – Goodbye!

Glossary

Andalucia A region in the south of Spain. Málaga is in Andalucia.

castanets A small musical instrument made from two curved pieces of hollow wood, clicked together between fingers and thumb.

Epiphany A festival held by Christians on 6 January.

fiesta A religious festival.

flamenco A traditional style of Spanish music and dance.

paella A typical Spanish dish of rice cooked with seafood, meat and vegetables.

Picasso A famous Spanish artist who died in 1973.

siesta An afternoon sleep, usually taken after lunch.

tapas Light snacks, such as chopped meats, seafood, olives and potatoes, usually eaten with drinks.

Index